Still MostlyTrue

Volume 2: Collected Stories
& Drawings of Brian Andreas

StoryPeople
Decorah

ISBN-13: 978-0-964266-01-8
ISBN-10: 0-9642660-1-6

StoryPeople
P.O. Box 7
Decorah, IA 52101
USA
563.382.8060
563.382.0263 FAX
800.476.7178

storypeople@storypeople.com
www.storypeople.com

First Edition: *May, 1994*
Second Edition: *June, 2005*

*Printed by the West Coast Print Center, Oakland, California
on 10% tree-free kenaf / 90% recycled, chlorine-free archival text paper*

To my sons, David Quinn & Matthew Shea, for their spirit, wild & exuberant as life itself, & again & always to the heart of my heart, Ellen Rockne, for her thought & compassion & the fine, bright starlight dancing in her eyes.

Other books by Brian Andreas available
from StoryPeople Press:

Mostly True
Going Somewhere Soon
Strange Dreams
Hearing Voices
Trusting Soul
Story People
Traveling Light

Still MostlyTrue

Introduction

I've always seen hidden meanings in everything. Whenever I used to do those puzzles in children's magazines, the ones where you're supposed to find all the hidden pictures, I'd never find the right ones. I'd say I found the griffin, and the Wesselman steam engine, and the missing little finger of the mummy of Tut, and everyone would give me a strange look and say, All you're looking for is a yellow duck.

I like to find the secrets hidden in the moments of everyday life. My grandmother used to tell us that once upon a time everything in the world had a voice, and every place you walked you could hear the whispers if you listened close enough. I believe the world still whispers. But we have forgotten how to listen.

Take some time to listen to the voices around you. Start some place easy, like in an old photo album. Listen to the sounds of your memories, like the voice of your great-grandmother at her ninetieth birthday party, or the sound of the waves at the beach that summer when you and your sister found the dried-up cat's paw.

After that, work up to the voices of places you can only imagine. Ask where to find the griffin, and the Wesselman steam engine, and the little finger of Tut. I know they're out there, and usually in the strangest of places.

And if you find the yellow duck, let me know. That's the one I always miss.

With love,

Brian Andreas

My grandmother
used to say life
was so much
easier when you
were simple-minded.

It's taken me
almost my whole
life to understand
what she meant.

After he was quiet
a long time, words
began to come to
him in dreams &
told him their
secret names & this
was the way he learned
the true nature of
 the world.

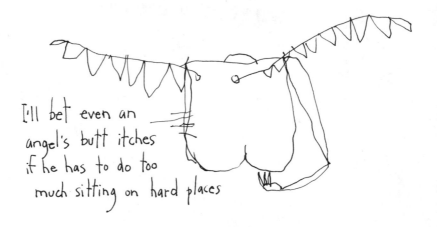

I'll bet even an
angel's butt itches
if he has to do too
much sitting on hard places

Secret Names

When I met the
Grandfather of
Time, he said
it was no use
struggling.

Even after all
these years he
still had too
much to do.

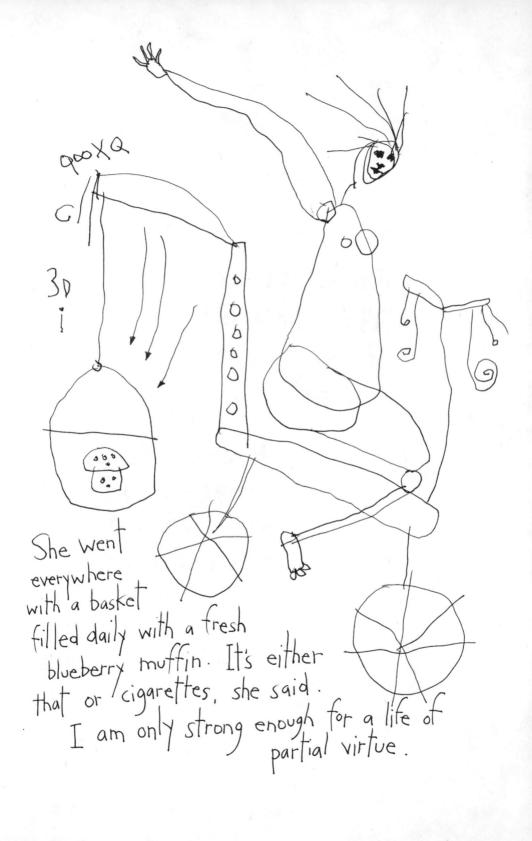

She went
everywhere
with a basket
filled daily with a fresh
blueberry muffin. It's either
that or cigarettes, she said.
I am only strong enough for a life of
partial virtue.

He told me once
that if I kept it
up long enough
I'd probably get
wise enough to
be silly in public,

but I probably
won't wait
that long.

Impatience

I'm not
so good
at taking
my own
advice,
she said,

but that
doesn't
mean I
don't know
what's right.

the singing on her belly dance
records reminded her of the
cattle auctions she used to
go to with her grandfather &
she would sing along softly,

fourfiftyfourfiftyfour
seventyfivegorgeous
gorgeousgorgeous myohmy,
she would say

& then she would raise her
hands above her head &
ripple her body like trees
in the wind.

Belly Dancer

He won the grand
prize of a vacuum
cleaner & all the
canned goods he
could carry &
when they told him
he couldn't believe
it.

I thought I was
buying drink tickets,
he said.

Winning Ticket

he wore the devil
costume at every
opportunity even though
the pants were too
short & could never
understand why
no one would
take him
seriously

She told me she
moved to LA so
she could dye her
hair & be in a band.

A couple of years
after that someone
told me she'd quit
her band to go to
cosmetology school.

I guess it was easier
to give up music than
to give up the hair.

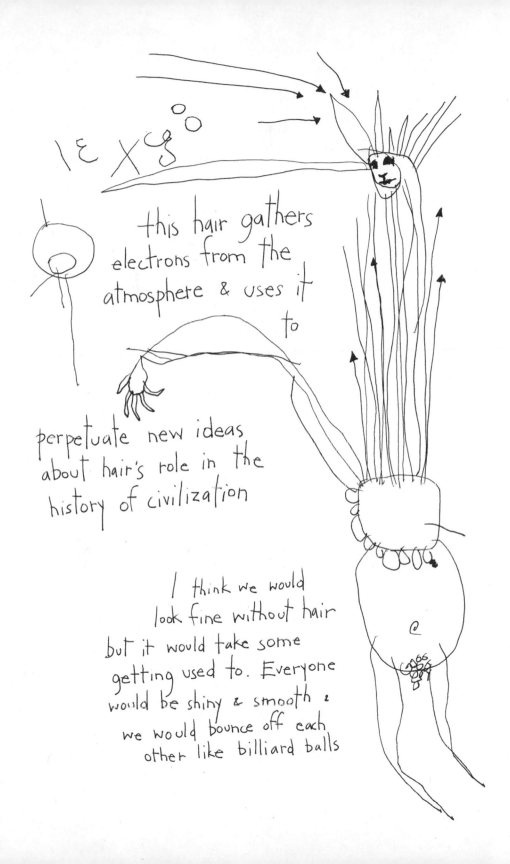

this hair gathers electrons from the atmosphere & uses it to

perpetuate new ideas about hair's role in the history of civilization

I think we would look fine without hair but it would take some getting used to. Everyone would be shiny & smooth & we would bounce off each other like billiard balls

these are teeth
in a box & it
swallows up all
the mean things
in the world & holds them in its
jaws until times start to change

If I was a spider princess,
she said, I would spin
webs the color of sky &
catch drops of sunlight
to give to children who
watch too much tv & then
everyone would remember
to come outside to play.

If I was a spider
princess, she said,
things would be
different.

You have
to remember
to make it all
over again every
day, the angel said
to me. Otherwise
it goes all
to hell.

I was waiting for the
longest time, she said.
I thought you forgot.

It is hard to forget, I
said, when there is
such an empty space
when you are gone.

She seemed to
move everywhere
dancing & music
followed her

  like

    leaves

      on

        the

         wind.

She said these legs have a mind of their own.
Once they kicked a salesperson in Nordstrom's
and she felt so bad, she bought almost $400
worth of stuff
& waited
almost a
week to
return it.

She is thinking of sending them to obedience school.
Their best trick is a judicious use of pantyhose.
Legs hate that kind of stuff so all it takes is one time.

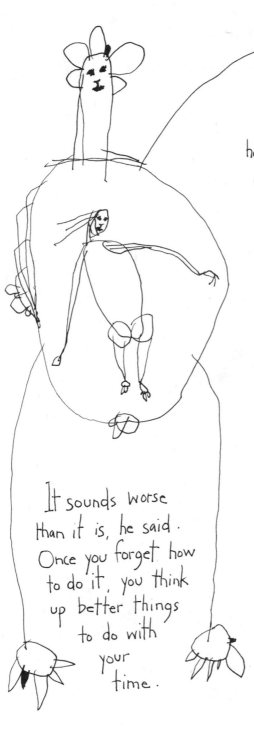

he said he was followed
around by a cloud of
electrons that knew
what he was
thinking.

I've given up
lying, he said &
then he pointed
over his shoulder.

What's the point?
They just go &
tell everybody the
truth anyway.

It sounds worse
than it is, he said.
Once you forget how
to do it, you think
up better things
to do with
your
time.

There are days
I drop words
of comfort on
myself like

    falling

      leaves

        & remember
        that it is
        enough to be
        taken care of
        by my self.

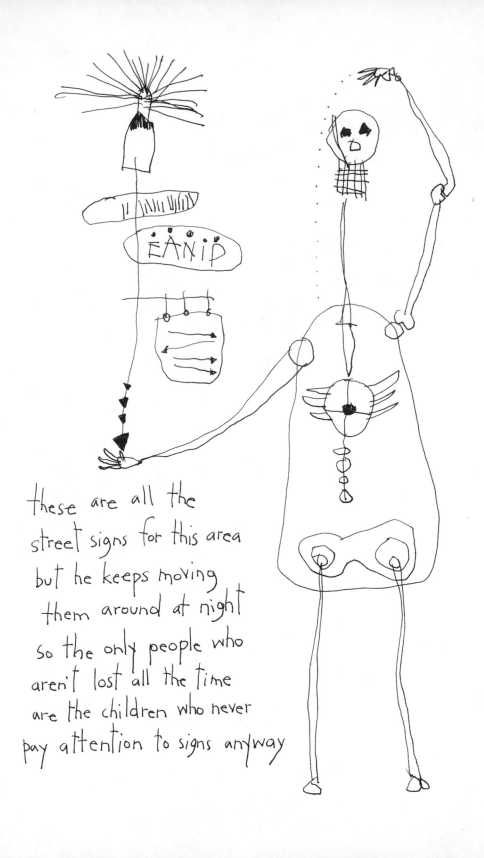

these are all the
street signs for this area
but he keeps moving
them around at night
so the only people who
aren't lost all the time
are the children who never
pay attention to signs anyway

Every day he stood in
front of the Bank of
America. You're
             trapped
               in the belly
                  of a big
                     pink pig,
                        he said.

We ignored him.
We had work to do.

Belly of the Pig

There are your fog
people & your sun
people, he said. I
said I wasn't sure
which kind I was.
He nodded. Fog'll
do that to you, he
said.

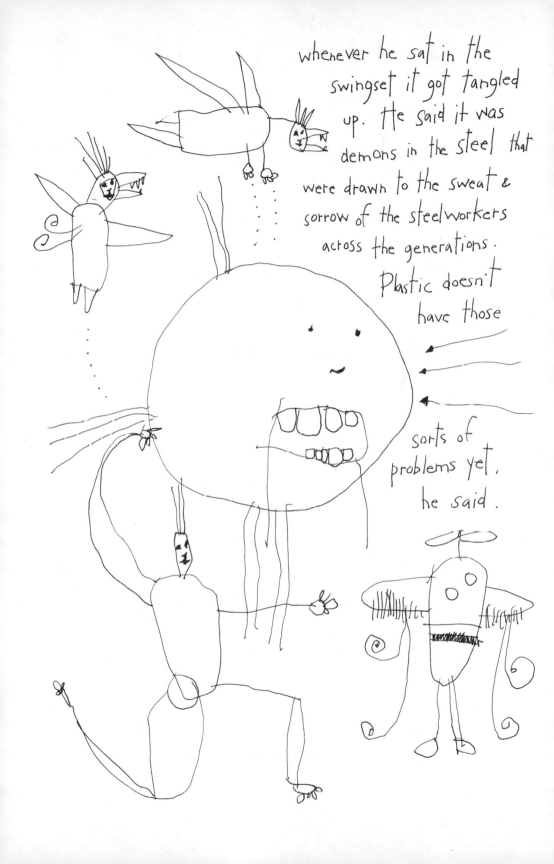

whenever he sat in the
swingset it got tangled
up. He said it was
demons in the steel that
were drawn to the sweat &
sorrow of the steelworkers
across the generations.
Plastic doesn't
have those

sorts of
problems yet,
he said.

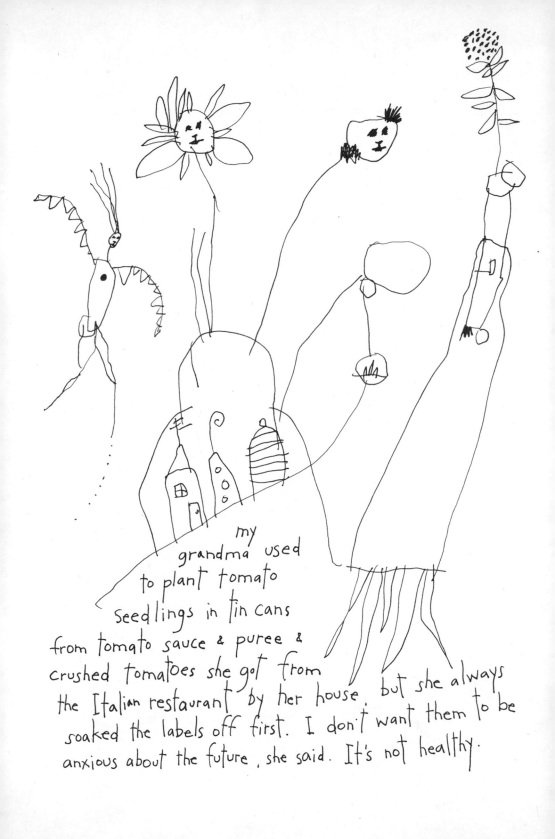

my
grandma used
to plant tomato
seedlings in tin cans
from tomato sauce & puree &
crushed tomatoes she got from
the Italian restaurant by her house, but she always
soaked the labels off first. I don't want them to be
anxious about the future, she said. It's not healthy.

I will
always remember
the day when the sun
shone dark on your hair
& I forgot where we
were & kissed you
lightly on the
nose

& suddenly
   there was no more secret.

The day he first told me he
was starting to disappear I
didn't believe him & so he stopped
& held his hand up to the sun & it
was like thin paper in the light &
finally I said. you seem very calm
for a man who is disappearing &
he said it was a relief after all
those years of trying to keep the
pieces of his life in one place.
Later on, I went to see him
again & as I was leaving, he
put a package in my hand.
   This is the last piece of my
life. he said. take good care
of it & then he smiled & was
gone & the room filled with the
sound of the wind & when I
opened the package there was
nothing there & I thought
there must be some mistake
or maybe I dropped it & I

got down on my hands &
knees & looked until the light
began to fade & then slowly
I felt pieces of my life
fall away & suddenly I
understood what he meant
& I lay there for a long
time crying & laughing at
the same time.

Disappearing

I dug up an anthill once & my friend told me
the ant gods would come to get me in my dreams
& I said I didn't believe him but later that
night

I went down & tried to put
the anthill back together & I even added some
lettuce & mashed potatoes & pork chop from
dinner in case they'd been too busy to eat & I
never heard from the ant gods so I figure
it worked out.

When I was 5, he said, my family forgot & left me at the fair. I wandered around in the bright sounds & smells of hot sawdust & cotton candy for hours. It was already too late by the time my parents found me.

I haven't been fit for decent society since.

he has a hole
where his
heart used to
be because
it fell out when he was running from scary
things one night in a dream & it hurts all the
time now & he doesn't know how to fix it &
sometimes I think he doesn't even remember
that it's gone.

She left pieces of her
life behind her
everywhere
she went.

It's easier
to feel the
sunlight
without them,
she said.

Leaving Pieces

Our mailman was a dance
teacher at night & I would
watch him sometimes to see if
he would deliver mail differently
than the others. I expected to see him leap
over bushes with his toes pointing like arrows,
but all he ever did was walk.

he told me about
Jesus & Arizona
& the best way to
make beer & I
said you're a
funny kind of
preacher & he
said it's a funny
kind of world & I
still remember his
eyes clear as a
desert morning

every night for a hundred
years the angel of dreams came to the
town & splashed the walls with bright
colors that stayed until the first light
of day

As long as the sun shall
rise goes the old lover's
vow. But we are children
of a scientific age & have
no time for poetry. Still,
I offer a quiet prayer of
thanks for the sunlight
each time I see your face.

The birds
brought seeds
& flowers & bits
of brightly colored
string & placed them in
her hair while she slept so
that she would remember
the wild joy of
spring
when she
finally
awoke.

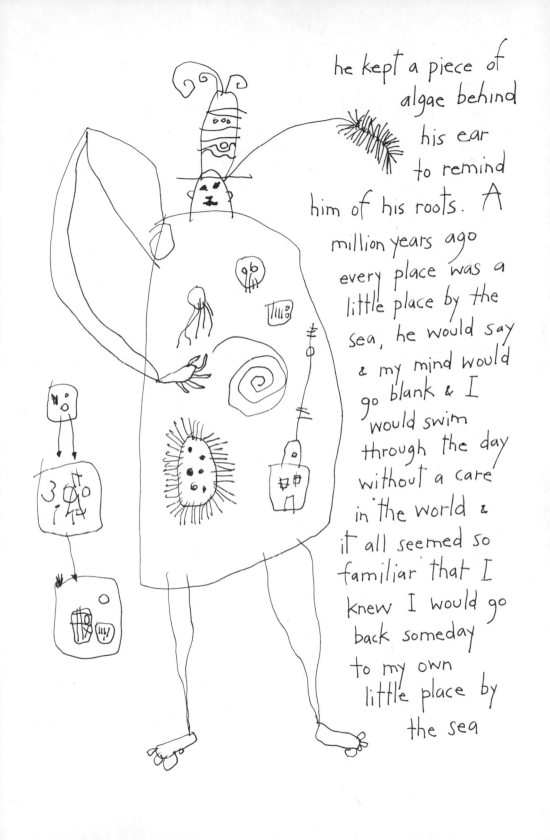

he kept a piece of
algae behind
his ear
to remind
him of his roots. A
million years ago
every place was a
little place by the
sea, he would say
& my mind would
go blank & I
would swim
through the day
without a care
in the world &
it all seemed so
familiar that I
knew I would go
back someday
to my own
little place by
the sea

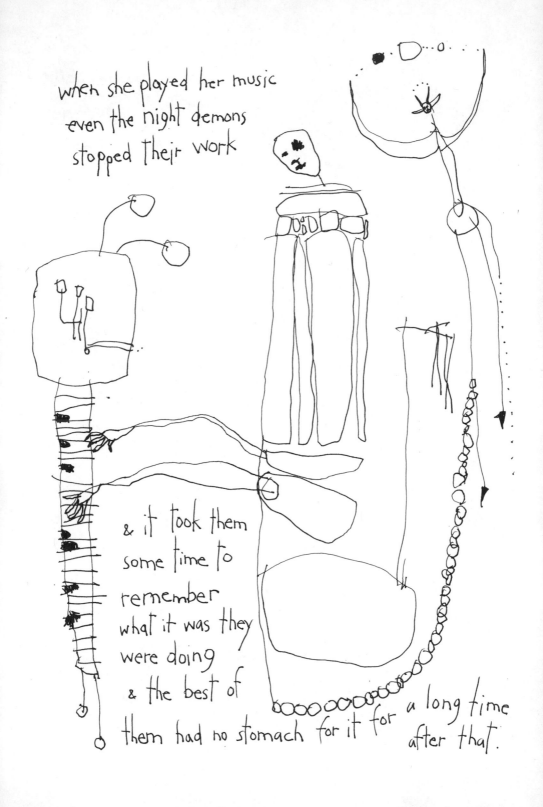

when she played her music
even the night demons
stopped their work

& it took them
some time to
remember
what it was they
were doing
& the best of
them had no stomach for it for a long time
after that.

we had gone
far enough
together to
listen easily
in the quiet
spaces

we used to go visit my
grandma on the train &
on the way my sister & I
would talk to people we
met & tell them we were
from Hawaii & could speak
Polynesian & I'd hold up a
7-Up & say this is called
puka-puka-wanini on the
Big Island & we'd make up
longer & longer names until
it took about 10 minutes
to say one & about that time
we would be there & we'd
say aloha & go off to have
lunch at my grandma's &
my sister would hold up a
Mrs. Paul's fish stick & say
in Hawaii they call these
molo-molo-pooey-pooey &
I'd try not to choke on
my fruit punch.

Native Hawaiians

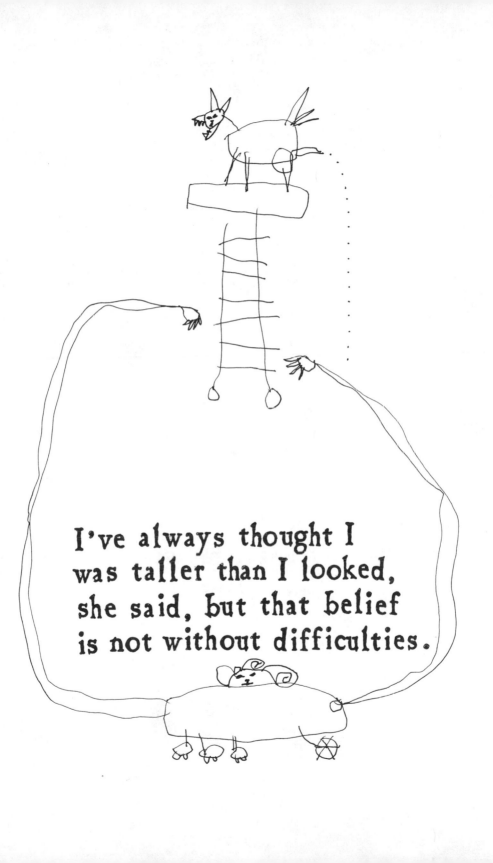

I've always thought I
was taller than I looked,
she said, but that belief
is not without difficulties.

The clock is a conspiracy
& a crime against humanity

& I would not
own one

except I miss
appointments
without it .

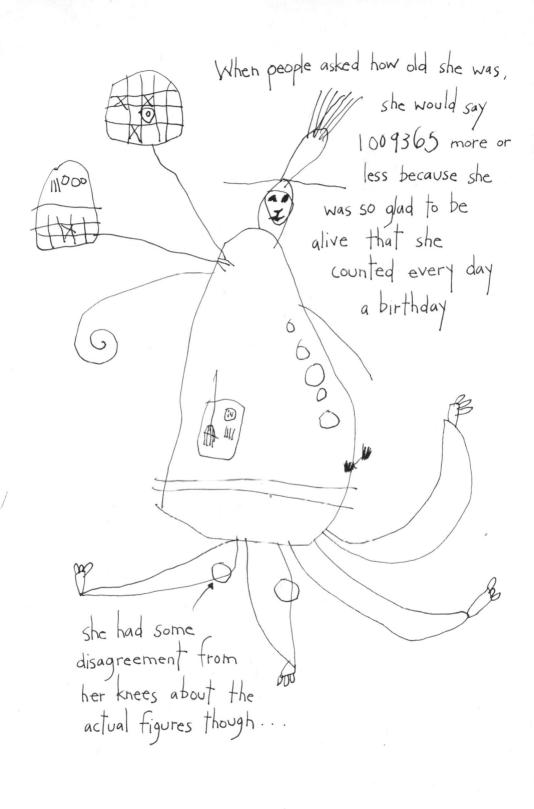

When people asked how old she was, she would say 1009365 more or less because she was so glad to be alive that she counted every day a birthday

she had some disagreement from her knees about the actual figures though . . .

1396 EGID

these are bowls filled with some kind of black goop.
My friend says it's the blood from the slaughterhouse
but why would they leave it where innocent people
could step in it? is what I said & he said that's
the way meateaters think.

The preacher dunked
her head 3 times in
the basin & called out
for the demons to
leave & then she spit
water in his face.

So he extemporaneously
added a fourth & by
the time she came up
for air the demons
were considerably
more restrained.

for a long time, he was trying to
pop these balloons with psychic energy
but he found a dart was simpler.
I save my psychic energy for
more   important things,
he told me,

like trying
to predict
the future.
I told him a dart is good for that
too & now he never calls anymore.

I have too much to lose,
she said, if I cross that
line.

   Like what? I said. She
   could not think of
   anything that day so she
   said she'd get back to me.

Since then I've been
thinking what I would
lose if I crossed my
line & I haven't come
up with anything either.

   There's always another
     line somewhere.

Crossing the Line

I think my life would be easier, he said, if I could just get my selves to agree on something.

The secret is
not in your
hand
   or your
   eye
     or your
     voice,
my aunt once
told me. The
secret is in
your heart.

Of course, she said, knowing
that doesn't make it any easier.

this is a pretty deep
hole for putting away all
the ugly things in the world.
For a long time it was empty,
but it started filling up
really fast the last couple
of years.

She saw herself
reflected in the
store window &
then the sun
changed & she
disappeared &
all she could
see was her eyes
& she remembered
thinking, I make
a very nice floor
lamp & that was
the day she decided
to quit her job.

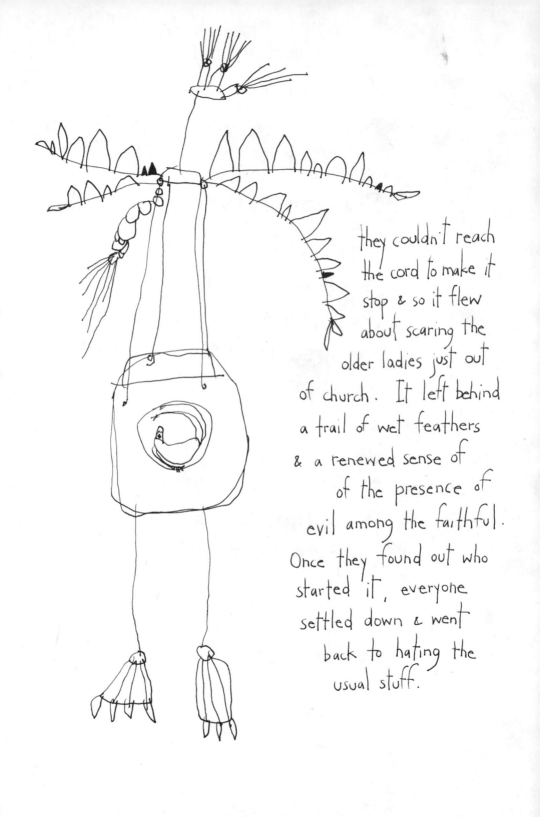

they couldn't reach
the cord to make it
stop & so it flew
about scaring the
older ladies just out
of church. It left behind
a trail of wet feathers
& a renewed sense of
of the presence of
evil among the faithful.
Once they found out who
started it, everyone
settled down & went
back to hating the
usual stuff.

most people don't
know there are
angels whose only
job is to make sure
you don't get too
comfortable & fall
asleep & miss your
life

this is a
monster in a
box & all it
eats is sugar
& raw hamburger
so you can
understand how
it got to be
so fierce

One day, he decided he
was more dependent on the
kindness of women than
he liked so he went off to
hunt wild beasts with his
bare hands. But all he found
was a stray dog & a couple
of old pigeons & it was
cold & he missed the sound
of soft voices,

so finally he came back &
never worried about it again.

Iron John

he wore a pot on his head in all
kinds of weather.
    I never learned
to cook & I got it

after my
mother died,
he said. I just
know it would
make her happy
that I'm using
it.

each night,
all the years we
were growing up,
she sat in the big
yellow rocking chair

  & pieced together
              our lives

    with countless
    stitches of her
    silver needle

I had vegetarians
in my past, she
said, but they're
gone now

& I'm a lot
happier.

Post Vegetarian

he is self-conscious because everyone knows he has wings but they've never seen him fly.

Now & then there will be a feather in odd places or maybe a footprint to show he was there.

All in all, he thinks it's nobody else's business what he does with his free time

There was a whole world
here once, she said, but
some of the smaller parts
left on personal business
& it's not that easy to
find replacements.

I was going to be
the solar system, she said,
but I kept getting caught
in the trees & bushes.

Every weekend, she
went to the city &
looked through the
bones of the dead for
old clothes & bits
of fashion jewelry.
She always seemed
a bit tattered, but
I didn't say much
about it. I was still
young & hadn't settled
on a past I was
comfortable with yet
either.

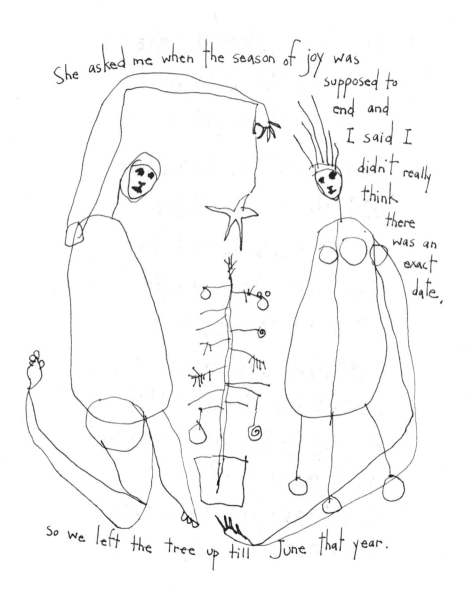

She asked me when the season of joy was supposed to end and I said I didn't really think there was an exact date,

So we left the tree up till June that year.

My grandmother
told me once
that a city has
enough windows
for everybody.

I still want to believe her.

She softened
gradually, melting
in the light of the
sun, all the while
thinking, O, this
is what it's like to
be a planet

           & suddenly
              it was over

& the universe expanded
by one.

Earth Mother

Death take me now &
spare me the pain, she
said. It was difficult
for me to get that
excited. Get a
grip, I said, it's
only aerobics.

they came to sit
& dangle their
feet off the edge
of the world

& after awhile
they forgot
everything but
the good & true
things they would
do someday

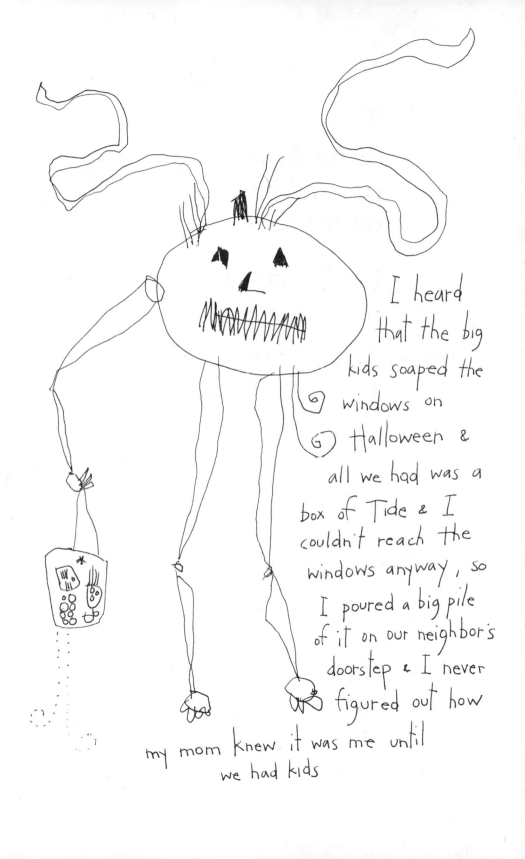

I heard
that the big
kids soaped the
windows on
Halloween &
all we had was a
box of Tide & I
couldn't reach the
windows anyway, so
I poured a big pile
of it on our neighbor's
doorstep & I never
figured out how
my mom knew it was me until
we had kids

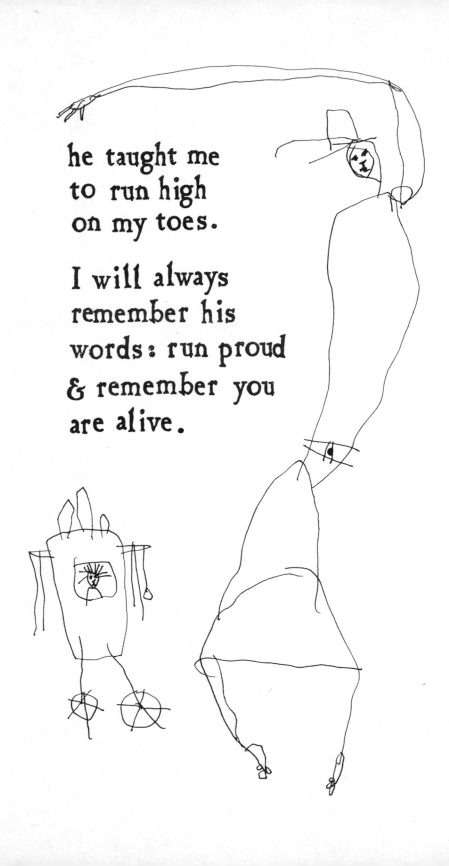

he taught me
to run high
on my toes.

I will always
remember his
words: run proud
& remember you
are alive.

In my dream,
the angel shrugged
& said, If we
fail this time, it
will be a failure of
imagination

& then she placed the world
gently in the palm of my hand.

About the Artist

Brian Andreas is an artist, sculptor, and storyteller, who works with new forms of human community. He uses traditional media from fine art, theatre and storytelling, as well as the latest electronic technologies of computer networks, virtual reality and multimedia. His work is shown and collected internationally.

Born in 1956 in Iowa City, Iowa, he holds a B.A. from Luther College in Decorah, Iowa, and an M.F.A. in Fiber and Mixed Media from John F. Kennedy University in Orinda, California.

After years of adventure on the West Coast, he now lives with his wife, Ellen Rockne, and their two wild and beautiful boys in Decorah, Iowa, where he continues to make new stories for the StoryPeople, and, of course, for his next book.

About StoryPeople

StoryPeople are wood sculptures, three to four feet tall, in a roughly human form. They can be as varied as a simple cutout figure, or an assemblage of found and scrap wood, or an intricate, roughly made treasure box. Each piece uses only recycled barn and fence wood from old homesteads in the northeast Iowa area. Adding to their individual quirkiness are scraps of old barn tin and twists of wire. They are painted with bright colors and hand-stamped a letter at a time (using the same stamp set that you see on the hand-stamped pages of this book), with original stories. The most striking aspect of StoryPeople are the shaded spirit faces. These faces are softly blended into the wood surface, and make each StoryPerson come alive.

Every figure is marked and numbered at the studio, and is unique because of the materials used. The figures, the colorful story prints, and the books, are available in galleries and stores throughout the US, Canada and the UK (along with a few others scattered about the world), and on our web site. Please feel free to call or write for more information, or drop in on the web at **www.storypeople.com**

StoryPeople
P.O. Box 7
Decorah, IA 52101
USA

800.476.7178
563.382.8060
563.382.0263 FAX

orders@storypeople.com